Instructional Guides for Literature

Sarah, Plain and Tall

A guide for the book by Patricia MacLachlan
Great Works Author: Kristi Sturgeon

Publishing Credits

Robin Erickson, *Production Director;* Lee Aucoin, *Creative Director;* Timothy J. Bradley, *Illustration Manager;* Emily R. Smith, M.A.Ed., *Editorial Director;* Amber Goff, *Editorial Assistant;* Don Tran, *Production Supervisor;* Corinne Burton, M.A.Ed., *Publisher*

Image Credits

Cover image MBoe/Donna Beeler/Shutterstock

Standards

Shell Education
5301 Oceanus Drive
Huntington Beach, CA 92649-1030
http://www.shelleducation.com

ISBN 978-1-4258-8970-8

Table of Contents

How to Use This Literature Guide

Today's standards demand rigor and relevance in the reading of complex texts. The units in this series guide teachers in a rich and deep exploration of worthwhile works of literature for classroom study. The most rigorous instruction can also be interesting and engaging!

Many current strategies for effective literacy instruction have been incorporated into these instructional guides for literature. Throughout the units, text-dependent questions are used to determine comprehension of the book as well as student interpretation of the vocabulary words. The books chosen for the series are complex and are exemplars of carefully crafted works of literature. Close reading is used throughout the units to guide students toward revisiting the text and using textual evidence to respond to prompts orally and in writing. Students must analyze the story elements in multiple assignments for each section of the book. All of these strategies work together to rigorously guide students through their study of literature.

The next few pages will make clear how to use this guide for a purposeful and meaningful literature study. Each section of this guide is set up in the same way to make it easier for you to implement the instruction in your classroom.

Theme Thoughts

The great works of literature used throughout this series have important themes that have been relevant to people for many years. Many of the themes will be discussed during the various sections of this instructional guide. However, it would also benefit students to have independent time to think about the key themes of the book.

Before students begin reading, have them complete the *Pre-Reading Theme Thoughts* (page 13). This graphic organizer will allow students to think about the themes outside the context of the story. They'll have the opportunity to evaluate statements based on important themes and defend their opinions. Be sure to keep students' papers for comparison to the *Post-Reading Theme Thoughts* (page 59). This graphic organizer is similar to the pre-reading activity. However, this time, students will be answering the questions from the point of view of one of the characters in the book. They have to think about how the character would feel about each statement and defend their thoughts. To conclude the activity, have students compare what they thought about the themes before the book to what the characters discovered during the story.

How to Use This Literature Guide *(cont.)*

Vocabulary

Each teacher reference vocabulary overview page has definitions and sentences about how key vocabulary words are used in the section. These words should be introduced and discussed with students. Students will use these words in different activities throughout the book.

On some of the vocabulary student pages, students are asked to answer text-related questions about vocabulary words from the sections. The following question stems will help you create your own vocabulary questions if you'd like to extend the discussion.

- How does this word describe _____'s character?
- How does this word connect to the problem in this story?
- How does this word help you understand the setting?
- Tell me how this word connects to the main idea of this story.
- What visual pictures does this word bring to your mind?
- Why do you think the author used this word?

At times, you may find that more work with the words will help students understand their meanings and importance. These quick vocabulary activities are a good way to further study the words.

- Students can play vocabulary concentration. Make one set of cards that have the words on them and another set with the definitions. Then, have students lay them out on the table and play concentration. The goal of the game is to match vocabulary words with their definitions. For early readers or English language learners, the sets of cards could be the words and pictures of the words.
- Students can create word journal entries about the words. Students choose words they think are important and then describe why they think each word is important within the book. Early readers or English language learners could instead draw pictures about the words in a journal.
- Students can create puppets and use them to act out the vocabulary words from the stories. Students may also enjoy telling their own character-driven stories using vocabulary words from the original stories.

How to Use This Literature Guide *(cont.)*

Analyzing the Literature

After you have read each section with students, hold a small-group or whole-class discussion. Provided on the teacher reference page for each section are leveled questions. The questions are written at two levels of complexity to allow you to decide which questions best meet the needs of your students. The Level 1 questions are typically less abstract than the Level 2 questions. These questions are focused on the various story elements, such as character, setting, and plot. Be sure to add further questions as your students discuss what they've read. For each question, a few key points are provided for your reference as you discuss the book with students.

Reader Response

In today's classrooms, there are often great readers who are below average writers. So much time and energy is spent in classrooms getting students to read on grade level that little time is left to focus on writing skills. To help teachers include more writing in their daily literacy instruction, each section of this guide has a literature-based reader response prompt. Each of the three genres of writing is used in the reader responses within this guide: narrative, informative/explanatory, and opinion. Before students write, you may want to allow them time to draw pictures related to the topic. Book-themed writing paper is provided on pages 69–70 if your students need more space to write.

Guided Close Reading

Within each section of this guide, it is suggested that you closely reread a portion of the text with your students. Page numbers are given, but since some versions of the books may have different page numbers, the sections to be reread are described by location as well. After rereading the section, there are a few text-dependent questions to be answered by students. A graphic organizer has been provided to help students prepare for the group discussion. They should record their thoughts and ideas on the graphic organizer and refer to it during your discussion. Rather than just taking notes, you may want to require students to write complete responses to the questions before discussing them with you.

Encourage students to read one question at a time and then go back to the text and discover the answer. Work with students to ensure that they use the text to determine their answers rather than making unsupported inferences. Suggested answers are provided in the answer key.

How to Use This Literature Guide *(cont.)*

Guided Close Reading *(cont.)*

The generic open-ended stems below can be used to write your own text-dependent questions if you would like to give students more practice.

- What words in the story support . . . ?
- What text helps you understand . . . ?
- Use the book to tell why _____ happens.
- Based on the events in the story, . . . ?
- Show me the part in the text that supports . . . .
- Use the text to tell why . . . .

Making Connections

The activities in this section help students make cross-curricular connections to mathematics, science, social studies, fine arts, or other curricular areas. These activities require higher-order thinking skills from students but also allow for creative thinking.

Language Learning

A special section has been set aside to connect the literature to language conventions. Through these activities, students will have opportunities to practice the conventions of standard English grammar, usage, capitalization, and punctuation.

Story Elements

It is important to spend time discussing what the common story elements are in literature. Understanding the characters, setting, plot, and theme can increase students' comprehension and appreciation of the story. If teachers begin discussing these elements in early childhood, students will more likely internalize the concepts and look for the elements in their independent reading. Another very important reason for focusing on the story elements is that students will be better writers if they think about how the stories they read are constructed.

In the story elements activities, students are asked to create work related to the characters, setting, or plot. Consider having students complete only one of these activities. If you give students a choice on this assignment, each student can decide to complete the activity that most appeals to him or her. Different intelligences are used so that the activities are diverse and interesting to all students.

How to Use This Literature Guide *(cont.)*

Culminating Activity

At the end of this instructional guide is a creative culminating activity that allows students the opportunity to share what they've learned from reading the book. This activity is open ended so that students can push themselves to create their own great works within your language arts classroom.

Comprehension Assessment

The questions in this section require students to think about the book they've read as well as the words that were used in the book. Some questions are tied to quotations from the book to engage students and require them to think about the text as they answer the questions.

Response to Literature

Finally, students are asked to respond to the literature by drawing pictures and writing about the characters and stories. A suggested rubric is provided for teacher reference.

Correlation to the Standards

Shell Education is committed to producing educational materials that are research and standards based. In this effort, we have correlated all of our products to the academic standards of all 50 United States, the District of Columbia, the Department of Defense Dependents Schools, and all Canadian provinces.

Purpose and Intent of Standards

Standards are designed to focus instruction and guide adoption of curricula. Standards are statements that describe the criteria necessary for students to meet specific academic goals. They define the knowledge, skills, and content students should acquire at each level. Standards are also used to develop standardized tests to evaluate students' academic progress. Teachers are required to demonstrate how their lessons meet standards. Standards are used in the development of all of our products, so educators can be assured they meet high academic standards.

How To Find Standards Correlations

To print a customized correlation report of this product for your state, visit our website at http://www.shelleducation.com and follow the online directions. If you require assistance in printing correlation reports, please contact Customer Service at 1-877-777-3450.

Correlation to the Standards *(cont.)*

Standards Correlation Chart

The lessons in this guide were written to support the Common Core College and Career Readiness Anchor Standards. This chart indicates which sections of this guide address the anchor standards.

Common Core College and Career Readiness Anchor Standard	Section
CCSS.ELA-Literacy.CCRA.R.1—Read closely to determine what the text says explicitly and to make logical inferences from it; cite specific textual evidence when writing or speaking to support conclusions drawn from the text.	Guided Close Reading Sections 1–5; Story Elements Sections 2, 4; Culminating Activity
CCSS.ELA-Literacy.CCRA.R.2—Determine central ideas or themes of a text and analyze their development; summarize the key supporting details and ideas.	Analyzing the Literature Sections 1–5; Guided Close Reading Sections 1–5; Making Connections Sections 1, 3–4; Story Elements Section 2; Culminating Activity; Post-Reading Response to Literature
CCSS.ELA-Literacy.CCRA.R.3—Analyze how and why individuals, events, or ideas develop and interact over the course of a text.	Analyzing the Literature Sections 1–5; Guided Close Reading Sections 1–5; Story Elements Sections 1–3, 5; Post-Reading Response to Literature
CCSS.ELA-Literacy.CCRA.R.4—Interpret words and phrases as they are used in a text, including determining technical, connotative, and figurative meanings, and analyze how specific word choices shape meaning or tone.	Vocabulary Sections 1–5; Guided Close Reading Sections 1–5
CCSS.ELA-Literacy.CCRA.R.5—Analyze the structure of texts, including how specific sentences, paragraphs, and larger portions of the text (e.g., a section, chapter, scene, or stanza) relate to each other and the whole.	Guided Close Reading Sections 1–5
CCSS.ELA-Literacy.CCRA.R.10—Read and comprehend complex literary and informational texts independently and proficiently.	Guided Close Reading Sections 1–5; Story Elements Section 4
CCSS.ELA-Literacy.CCRA.W.1—Write arguments to support claims in an analysis of substantive topics or texts using valid reasoning and relevant and sufficient evidence.	Guided Close Reading Sections 1–5; Reader Response Section 3; Culminating Activity
CCSS.ELA-Literacy.CCRA.W.2—Write informative/explanatory texts to examine and convey complex ideas and information clearly and accurately through the effective selection, organization, and analysis of content.	Reader Response Sections 2, 5; Post-Reading Response to Literature
CCSS.ELA-Literacy.CCRA.W.3—Write narratives to develop real or imagined experiences or events using effective technique, well-chosen details and well-structured event sequences.	Reader Response Sections 1, 4; Post-Reading Response to Literature

Correlation to the Standards *(cont.)*

Standards Correlation Chart *(cont.)*

Common Core College and Career Readiness Anchor Standard	Section
CCSS.ELA-Literacy.CCRA.W.4—Produce clear and coherent writing in which the development, organization, and style are appropriate to task, purpose, and audience.	Guided Close Reading Sections 1–5; Story Elements Section 1; Making Connections Section 2; Culminating Activity
CCSS.ELA-Literacy.CCRA.L.1—Demonstrate command of the conventions of standard English grammar and usage when writing or speaking.	Guided Close Reading Sections 1–5; Language Learning Sections 1, 3–5; Story Elements Section 1; Culminating Activity
CCSS.ELA-Literacy.CCRA.L.2—Demonstrate command of the conventions of standard English capitalization, punctuation, and spelling when writing.	Guided Close Reading Sections 1–5; Language Learning Section 2; Story Elements Section 1; Culminating Activity
CCSS.ELA-Literacy.CCRA.L.3—Apply knowledge of language to understand how language functions in different contexts, to make effective choices for meaning or style, and to comprehend more fully when reading or listening.	Guided Close Reading Sections 1–5; Making Connections Section 2
CCSS.ELA-Literacy.CCRA.L.4—Determine or clarify the meaning of unknown and multiple-meaning words and phrases by using context clues, analyzing meaningful word parts, and consulting general and specialized reference materials, as appropriate.	Vocabulary Section 1–5; Guided Close Reading Section 5
CCSS.ELA-Literacy.CCRA.L.5—Demonstrate understanding of figurative language, word relationships, and nuances in word meanings.	Making Connections Section 2; Response to Literature Sections 4–5
CCSS.ELA-Literacy.CCRA.L.6—Acquire and use accurately a range of general academic and domain-specific words and phrases sufficient for reading, writing, speaking, and listening at the college and career readiness level; demonstrate independence in gathering vocabulary knowledge when encountering an unknown term important to comprehension or expression.	Vocabulary Sections 1–5; Making Connections Section 1

TESOL and WIDA Standards

The lessons in this book promote English language development for English language learners. The following TESOL and WIDA English Language Development Standards are addressed through the activities in this book:

- **Standard 1:** English language learners communicate for social and instructional purposes within the school setting.
- **Standard 2:** English language learners communicate information, ideas and concepts necessary for academic success in the content area of language arts.

About the Author—Patricia MacLachlan

Patricia MacLachlan is an American children's author who is best known for her Newbery Medal-winning novel *Sarah, Plain and Tall.* She writes both picture books and novels. MacLachlan was born on March 3, 1938, in Wyoming. Although she has lived in Massachusetts most of her life, she still feels a strong connection to the prairie, which is evident in several of her books.

When writing, MacLachlan says she doesn't think of topics first, she thinks of characters. She begins having conversations with her characters and a story develops from there. She encourages young children who want to be writers to become readers first. MacLachlan recommends writing every single day. Most of her themes center on family and realism, and many readers can relate to her books.

MacLachlan currently lives in Massachusetts with her husband and two border terriers. She is a board member of the National Children's Book and Literacy Alliance, a non-profit organization that advocates for literacy, literature, and libraries.

Possible Texts for Text Comparisons

There are two other books in this trilogy written by Patricia MacLachlan: *Skylark* and *Caleb's Story*. Two additional books, by MacLachlan, were written as a continuation of the original series. They are *More Perfect than the Moon* and *Grandfather's Dance.*

Book Summary of *Sarah, Plain and Tall*

Anna misses her mother very much. Anna's mother died the day after Caleb, her brother, was born. This is especially hard for Caleb to understand. He constantly asks Anna about his mother and she tells him stories and about how she loved to sing. Papa used to sing, but he doesn't sing anymore.

The Witting family lives on a prairie in Kansas. Anna instantly becomes both a mother and sister to Caleb. The children are happy to hear their father has placed an advertisement for a wife. They have missed a motherly figure in their life.

A woman named Sarah responds to the advertisement and all three Wittings write back with excitement. They are thrilled when she agrees to come for a month to see how things go. They are nervous she will not stay long, that she will miss home too much, or that prairie life is not for her.

Sarah arrives and is independent, friendly, and hardworking. She brings memorabilia from home and gifts for the children. She teaches them new things and everyone loves having her around. As they get to know Sarah, the question of whether or not she will stay remains in their thoughts.

Cross-Curricular Connection

This book can be used in a social studies unit on geography or concepts of time (past and present). It can also be used to illustrate and teach letter writing.

Possible Texts for Text Sets

- Bannatyne-Cugnet, Jo. *A Prairie Alphabet*. Tundra Books, 2009.
- Bouchard, David. *If You're Not from the Prairie*. Aladdin, 1998.
- Bunting, Eve. *Dandelions*. HMH Books for Young Readers, 2001.
- Wilder, Laura Ingalls. *Little House on the Prairie*. HarperCollins, 2008.

Name ______________________ Date ____________

Pre-Reading Theme Thoughts

Directions: Draw a picture of a happy face or a sad face. Your face should show how you feel about each statement. Then, use words to say what you think about each statement.

Statement	How Do You Feel? ☺ ☹	What Do You Think?
It's exciting to try new things.		
Family is the most important thing in life.		
It's fun when things change in my life.		
I worry about people leaving.		

Vocabulary Overview

Key words and phrases from this section are provided below with definitions and sentences about how the words are used in the story. Introduce and discuss these important vocabulary words with students. If you think these words or other words in the story warrant more time devoted to them, there are suggestions in the introduction for other vocabulary activities (page 5).

Word	Definition	Sentence about Text
dusk (ch. 1)	partial darkness between day and night	It is **dusk**, and the dogs lay beside Caleb on the warm hearthstones.
hollow (ch. 1)	not solid; empty	The chair makes a **hollow** scraping sound on the hearthstones.
wretched (ch. 1)	terrible; very bad	Anna thought Caleb looked **wretched** when he was born.
feisty (ch. 1)	full of energy; troublesome; difficult	Papa's horse, Jack, is a **feisty** animal.
advertisement (ch. 1)	a paid announcement; a public notice	Papa places an **advertisement** in the newspaper for a new wife.
shingle (ch. 2)	a thin piece of wood, slate, or metal laid in rows to cover the roofs of buildings	Sarah describes her house as tall with gray **shingles.**
pitchfork (ch. 2)	a large, long-handled fork used for lifting hay	Papa stops cleaning the stalls and leans on his **pitchfork**.
grin (ch. 2)	to smile	Anna **grins** as she tells her father to say yes to Sarah's letter.
damp (ch. 2)	slightly wet; moist	It is rainy and the house is cool, **damp**, and quiet.
bonnet (ch. 2)	a hat, usually tying under the chin	Sarah writes that she will wear a yellow **bonnet**.

Name ______________________ Date ____________

Vocabulary Activity

Directions: Choose at least two words from the story. Draw a picture that shows what these words mean. Label your picture.

Words from the Story				
dusk	hollow	wretched	feisty	advertisement
shingle	bonnet	grin	damp	pitchfork

Directions: Answer this question.

1. Who will be wearing a yellow **bonnet** at the train station?

____

Analyzing the Literature

Provided below are discussion questions you can use in small groups, with the whole class, or for written assignments. Each question is written at two levels so you can choose the right question for each group of students. For each question, a few key points are provided for your reference as you discuss the book with students.

Story Element	Level 1	Level 2	Key Discussion Points
Character	What does Caleb continually ask Anna?	How does Anna feel when Caleb keeps asking about Mama and her singing?	Caleb continually asks Anna if Mama used to sing every day. Anna feels frustrated (as she's told him a hundred times this year!) and a bit sad remembering her mother.
Character	What does Anna not tell Caleb about his birth story?	Why doesn't Anna tell Caleb what she really thought of him when he was born?	Anna doesn't tell him he was homely and plain and smelled terrible. She doesn't tell him because it will hurt his feelings.
Plot	What unexpected news does Papa share after dinner?	How do you think the children feel after Papa's announcement?	Papa tells the children he put an advertisement for a wife in the newspaper. They are intrigued and happy at the thought of having a mother figure again.
Setting	Describe the children's home and surroundings.	How is the Witting home different from Sarah's home and surroundings?	Their home is small and surrounded by fields and grass. Sarah's house is tall and she lives near the sea.

Name ______________________ Date ____________

Reader Response

Think

Think about ways that you help others in your life.
What kinds of things do you do for them?

Narrative Writing Prompt

Anna has to work hard to take care of her brother and father. Tell about a time that you have helped to take care of someone.

Name ______________________ Date ______________

Guided Close Reading

Closely reread the last two pages of chapter 2. Start where it says, "One morning, early, Papa and Caleb . . . ." Read to the end of the chapter.

Directions: Think about these questions. In the chart, write ideas as you think about the answers. Be ready to share your answers.

1. What text supports the idea that the Witting family is excited to ask Sarah to visit?
2. Find the part in the story that describes how the family feels while waiting for Sarah's reply.
3. Use the text to tell why Papa smiles before holding up the letter for the children to see.

Name ______________________ Date ____________

Making Connections–Sea vs. Prairie

Sarah is from Maine, an East Coast state near the ocean. She loves living near the sea, but she feels it's time for a change. The Witting family lives on a prairie in Kansas, a Midwest state, far from the ocean. There are similarities and differences with both settings and ways of life.

Directions: Fill in the T-chart. Use details from chapters 1 and 2 as well as your own prior knowledge. Write the differences on the sides of the chart.

Sea	Prairie

Name ______________________ Date ______________

Language Learning–Writing Friendly Letters

Directions: Write a letter to Sarah. Tell her something unique about yourself. Describe where you live. Ask her at least two questions about herself.

Language Hints!

- Use a comma after your greeting.
- Use a comma after your closing.
- Indent your paragraphs.

Name ______________________ Date ____________

Story Elements–Setting

Directions: Draw a picture of what you think Sarah's home looks like in Maine. Also, draw a picture of the Witting's home on the prairie in Kansas.

Sarah's Home

Witting Home

Name ______________________ Date ____________

Story Elements–Plot

Directions: Make a prediction about how the children will react when they see Sarah for the first time. Sketch a scene and add some dialogue bubbles. What will they think? What will they say to her? What will their facial expressions look like?

Vocabulary Overview

Key words and phrases from this section are provided below with definitions and sentences about how the words are used in the story. Introduce and discuss these important vocabulary words with students. If you think these words or other words in the story warrant more time devoted to them, there are suggestions in the introduction for other vocabulary activities (page 5).

Word	Definition	Sentence about Text
bloom (ch. 3)	the state of flowers opening from buds	Sarah arrives through fields that **bloom** with colorful flowers.
hitch (ch. 3)	to harness an animal to a vehicle	Papa **hitches** the horses to the wagon.
stalls (ch. 3)	stables or sheds for horses or cattle	Caleb and Anna shovel out the **stalls**.
windmill (ch. 3)	a machine driven by the force of the wind, used for pumping or grinding	The wagon passes the **windmill** and the barn as Papa and Sarah arrive.
clatter (ch. 3)	a loud, rattling sound	The wagon **clatters** into the yard and stops by the steps.
blue flax (ch. 3)	a slender plant with blue flowers	Sarah's room is decorated with **blue flax** dried in a vase.
roamer (ch. 4)	one who wanders; travels with no purpose	Sarah's cat, Seal, is a **roamer** who never sleeps in one place.
scatter (ch. 4)	to throw loosely about; to separate	Sarah **scatters** Caleb's hair on the fence and ground.
rustle (ch.4)	to make slight, soft sounds	The children sit on the porch listening to the **rustle** of cows in the grass.
meadowlark (ch. 4)	American songbirds having a brownish and black back and wings and a yellow chest	Out in a field, a **meadowlark** sings.

Name ______________________ Date ____________

Vocabulary Activity

Directions: Draw lines to match the sentences.

Beginnings of the Sentences	Ends of the Sentences
The wagon passes the **windmill**	sings, too.
Out in a field, a **meadowlark**	Caleb's hair on the ground.
Papa feeds the horses as he	and the barn.
Sarah **scatters**	**blue flax** in a vase.
Sarah's room is decorated with	**hitches** them up to the wagon.

Directions: Answer this question.

1. What chores are done in the **stalls**?

____

____

Analyzing the Literature

Provided below are discussion questions you can use in small groups, with the whole class, or for written assignments. Each question is written at two levels so you can choose the right question for each group of students. For each question, a few key points are provided for your reference as you discuss the book with students.

Story Element	Level 1	Level 2	Key Discussion Points
Character	What does Papa wear when he picks up Sarah?	Why does Papa wear his good clothes to pick up Sarah?	Papa slicks back his hair and wears a clean blue shirt and a belt instead of suspenders. He wants to look his best and make a good first impression.
Plot	What chores do Caleb and Anna do after Papa leaves?	Why do the children do their chores without talking?	They shovel out the stalls, lay down new hay, feed the sheep, sweep, and carry wood and water. They do not want to waste time talking. They want to make sure the chores are done before Papa arrives with Sarah.
Setting	What does Sarah keep on her windowsill?	Why do you think Sarah keeps her shells on the windowsill?	Sarah keeps her shell collection on the windowsill as a daily reminder of her home.
Plot	What is Anna worried about at the end of chapter 3?	What makes Anna think Sarah is already lonely?	Anna is worried that Sarah is already lonely and won't stay long. Anna sees that she isn't smiling when she talks about the rolling land of the prairie.

Name ______________________ Date ______________

Reader Response

Think

Think about a time when you have traveled somewhere. It might have been far away, or maybe it was nearby.

Informative/Explanatory Writing Prompt

Describe how to prepare for a trip. What are some important steps you have to take?

Name ______________________ Date ____________

Guided Close Reading

Closely reread the part where Sarah cuts and styles the family's hair. It starts with, "At dusk Sarah cut . . ." and ends with, "Sarah's daughter."

Directions: Think about these questions. In the chart, write ideas or draw pictures as you think. Be ready to share your answers.

1. Use the book to tell why Sarah scatters the hair on the fence and ground.
2. Based on the events in the story, why does Papa go behind the barn to toss his pieces of hair into the wind?
3. Use the text to describe Anna and Sarah's relationship.

Name ______________________ Date ______________

Making Connections–Flower Fun

Sarah names three of the flowers that bloom in Maine: seaside goldenrod, wild asters, and woolly ragwort. Caleb thinks woolly ragwort has a funny name and proceeds to make up a song about it.

Directions: Fill in the missing words to make up your own song about your favorite flower. Add an illustration of your favorite flower next to your song.

I see a ________________________

growing in the ground.

It has colors of

____

all around.

It smells so good and looks

like ______________________.

I just might use it to

______________________________.

Name ____________________ Date ____________

Language Learning–Capitalization

Directions: The words on this page are all found in this section of *Sarah, Plain and Tall*. Rewrite them in alphabetical order. For each word, decide if you need to capitalize the word.

Language Hints!

- Capitalize people's names and geographic places.
- Start alphabetizing with the first letter of each word.

Words from the Section	Alphabetize
sarah	____________
dirt	____________
horses	____________
caleb	____________
shells	____________
russian	____________
wagon	____________
prairie	____________
anna	____________
maine	____________

Name ______________________ Date ____________

Story Elements–Setting

Directions: Create a map of the Wittings' land. Include the following items in your map. Include other items that you read about, as well. Each one needs a symbol that is in the map key.

- house
- barn
- stalls
- windmill
- wagon
- horses

Name ____________________ Date ____________

Story Elements–Plot

Directions: Singing is very important to the Witting family. They sing a song about summer in chapter 4. Write a song about your favorite season.

My Favorite Season

Vocabulary Overview

Key words and phrases from this section are provided below with definitions and sentences about how the words are used in the story. Introduce and discuss these important vocabulary words with students. If you think these words or other words in the story warrant more time devoted to them, there are suggestions in the introduction for other vocabulary activities (page 5).

Word	Definition	Sentence about Text
coarse (ch. 5)	not smooth; rough	Sarah feels the **coarse** wool of the sheep.
lantern (ch. 5)	a portable light in a closed case	Papa uses his **lantern** when he buries the sheep.
dune (ch. 5)	a sand hill formed by the wind	Sarah tells the children about how she used to slide down sand **dunes** with her brother.
canvas (ch. 5)	heavy cloth made of cotton, hemp, or linen	Papa covers a mound of hay with **canvas** to keep it dry.
plow (ch. 6)	cutting, lifting, or turning over soil	Papa teaches Sarah how to **plow** the fields.
frown (ch. 6)	an unhappy or angry facial expression	Anna **frowns** thinking about how she has to wait for winter, her favorite season.
tumbleweeds (ch. 6)	dried plants detached from the roots and blowing in the wind	Caleb tells Sarah how the winter winds bring **tumbleweeds**.
gully (ch. 6)	a ditch or gutter	Caleb runs and jumps over rocks and **gullies**.
startled (ch. 6)	to be surprised or shocked	The cows look **startled** as Sarah and the children swim in the cow pond.
wade (ch. 6)	to walk in water; partially submerged in water	Sarah **wades** in the cow pond, waiting for the children to join her.

Name ______________________ Date ____________

Vocabulary Activity

Directions: Each of these sentences contains a word from the story. Cut apart these sentence strips. Put the sentences in order based on the events in the story.

Caleb tells Sarah about the **tumbleweeds** that come during the winter.

Caleb runs and jumps over rocks and **gullies**.

Papa teaches Sarah how to **plow** the fields.

Sarah **wades** in the cow pond.

Papa uses his **lantern** when he buries the sheep.

Analyzing the Literature

Provided below are discussion questions you can use in small groups, with the whole class, or for written assignments. Each question is written at two levels so you can choose the right question for each group of students. For each question, a few key points are provided for your reference as you discuss the book with students.

Story Element	Level 1	Level 2	Key Discussion Points
Character	Why is Sarah so sad when she finds a lamb that has died?	What clues from the story let you know Sarah doesn't want to leave the dead sheep?	Sarah is sad because she had just bonded with the sheep, petting them, naming them, and singing to them. She stays there until night, when Papa comes to bury the dead sheep.
Plot	Why does Jacob make the dune for Sarah?	How does it make Sarah feel when Jacob makes the dune?	Jacob wants Sarah to feel at home; he is trying to make her happy. Sarah feels happy, as she is smiling and laughing as she slides down the dune three times.
Plot	What does Sarah draw pictures of?	Why does Sarah draw pictures to send home to Maine?	Sarah draws pictures of fields, sheep, the windmill, Papa, and the children. Drawing pictures is Sarah's way of describing her new home and surroundings to her family in Maine.
Character	What does Anna do while she lies on the grass after swimming?	What makes Anna's dream perfect?	Anna lies down to dry off and dreams. Anna's dream is perfect because in her dream, Sarah is happy.

Name ______________________ Date ____________

Reader Response

Think

Think about a time when you have had to learn something new. Also, think about all the things Sarah has to learn on the farm.

Opinion Writing Prompt

Sarah has to learn many new things. Give your opinion about this statement: *Learning new things is easy.*

____

____

____

____

____

____

____

____

____

____

____

____

Name ______________________ Date ____________

Guided Close Reading

Closely reread the section in chapter 5 where they all slide down the dune. Start with, "Next to the barn was . . . ." Continue reading until the end of the chapter.

Directions: Think about these questions. In the chart, write ideas or draw pictures as you think. Be ready to share your answers.

1. In what way does Papa make sure they will land safely at the bottom of the dune?
2. What words in this scene support the idea that they are becoming more like a real family?
3. What text supports the idea that Sarah may still not be settled yet?

Name ______________________ Date ____________

Making Connections–Mammals

Directions: Animals are important to the characters in this story. The most-referenced animals are horses, sheep, a cat, and dogs. All of these animals are mammals. Make a list of traits that all mammals share.

______________________ ______________________

______________________ ______________________

______________________ ______________________

Directions: Now, create your own mammal. You have to give it all the mammal traits you listed above. Be sure to give your unique mammal a special name.

Name ____________________ Date ____________

Language Learning–Adjectives

Directions: Compare and contrast winter in this book with winter where you live. Describe it with at least five adjectives in each column. At the bottom of each column, draw a picture of winter in each location.

Language Hints!

- Adjectives describe nouns.
- Common types of adjectives are colors, numbers, sounds, shapes, and weather.

• ____________	• ____________
• ____________	• ____________
• ____________	• ____________
• ____________	• ____________
• ____________	• ____________

Name ______________________ Date ____________

Story Elements–Setting

Directions: Sarah draws a picture of the fields. She sits looking at her picture for a long time before saying, "Something is missing." Draw the fields yourself and be sure to include what you think is missing from Sarah's picture.

Name ______________________ Date ____________

Story Elements–Plot

Directions: Papa teaches Sarah how to plow the fields. Sarah teaches Caleb how to swim. Describe three things that someone has taught you. Include a picture for each lesson you've learned.

Vocabulary Overview

Key words and phrases from this section are provided below with definitions and sentences about how the words are used in the story. Introduce and discuss these important vocabulary words with students. If you think these words or other words in the story warrant more time devoted to them, there are suggestions in the introduction for other vocabulary activities (page 5).

Word	Definition	Sentence about Text
whicker (ch. 7)	a whine; a whimper	The dogs **whicker** at the new horses.
shuffle (ch. 7)	to walk without lifting the feet	The chickens **shuffle** in the dirt.
quilt (ch. 7)	a bed cover stitched with patterns	Sarah and Maggie cover the table with a **quilt**.
squawk (ch. 7)	to make a loud, harsh sound	Sarah compares her aunts to **squawking** crows.
overalls (ch. 8)	loose pants with a bib and shoulder straps	Sarah dresses in a pair of **overalls**.
sly (ch. 8)	clever; mischievous	Papa's horse is **sly**.
rumble (ch. 8)	a deep, heavy, muffled sound	The thunder **rumbles** from the clouds.
squall (ch. 8)	a sudden, violent gust of wind	Sarah mentions they have **squalls** in Maine, too.
pungent (ch. 8)	a strong taste or smell; overpowering taste or smell	There is a **pungent** smell as soon as the storm hits.
eerie (ch. 8)	creepy; scary	The barn is **eerie** and very dark.

Name ______________________ Date ____________

Vocabulary Activity

Directions: Complete each sentence below with one of the vocabulary words listed here.

Words from the Story

whicker	shuffle	quilt	squawk	overalls
pungent	rumble	sly	eerie	squall

1. Sarah puts on Papa's ______________________ before heading into the barn.

2. Papa says Jack is too ______________________ and doesn't want Sarah riding him.

3. The chickens ______________________ across the dirt.

4. The storm brings on a ______________________ smell and a strong wind.

Directions: Answer this question.

5. What about the barn is dark and **eerie**?

____

____

Analyzing the Literature

Provided below are discussion questions you can use in small groups, with the whole class, or for written assignments. Each question is written at two levels so you can choose the right question for each group of students. For each question, a few key points are provided for your reference as you discuss the book with students.

Story Element	Level 1	Level 2	Key Discussion Points
Character	What does Maggie give Sarah "for eating"?	How does Anna know the chickens would not be for eating?	Maggie brings chickens for Sarah to eventually prepare and eat. Anna immediately knows that Sarah will befriend the animals and never eat them.
Plot	What does Sarah want to learn to do by herself?	Why do Anna and Caleb worry about Sarah learning how to do more on her own?	Sarah wants to ride a horse, drive a wagon, and go into town by herself. Anna and Caleb worry that she will leave if she knows how to ride and drive by herself.
Setting	What does the ground look like the morning after the storm?	Why do you think the ice-covered ground is compared to the sea?	The ground is covered in ice, from the hail. It is white and gleaming. It is compared to the sea because Sarah is becoming more and more at home, finding some similarities between her past and present lives.
Plot	Why do Jacob and Sarah run back out into the storm?	What does it say about Jacob when he runs out with Sarah to get the chickens?	They run back into the storm to get the chickens. Jacob genuinely cares for Sarah and wants to make sure she gets back to the barn safely as well as help her to save the animals that she loves.

Name ______________________ Date ____________

Reader Response

Think

Think about times that you have seen storms. It might have rained or snowed. Maybe it was just a strong wind.

Narrative Writing Prompt

In this section, the characters deal with a large snowstorm. Write about a time you have experienced a storm.

Name ______________________ Date ____________

Guided Close Reading

Closely reread the first few pages of chapter 8. Stop when Sarah says, "Remember, I told you?"

Directions: Think about these questions. In the chart, write ideas or draw pictures as you think. Be ready to share your answers.

1. What text helps you understand Sarah's mood?
2. Find evidence to support how Caleb feels about Sarah going into town by herself.
3. Use the book to tell why Sarah insisted, "*We* will fix the roof."

Name _______________________ Date ______________

Making Connections–Designing a Quilt

Directions: Sarah and Maggie use a quilt to cover the outside table for their picnic. Quilts can be simple or very detailed. Patchwork quilts are made up of small squares. Design a patchwork quilt that shows scenes and/or symbols from the story.

Name ______________________ Date ____________

Language Learning–Dialogue

Directions: Pretend that you are going to visit Anna and Caleb. Write a discussion you might have during your visit. Remember the rules of dialogue.

Language Hints!

- Use quotation marks around what is said.
- Use a comma to separate the quotation from the rest of the sentence.

Name ______________________ Date ____________

Story Elements–Characters

Directions: When the family runs into the barn to get out of the storm, Sarah unpacks a bag of cheese, bread, jam, and her shells. Make a list of ten items you would grab in an emergency situation, and explain why you chose each of those items.

- ____
- ____
- ____
- ____
- ____
- ____
- ____
- ____
- ____
- ____

Name ______________________ Date ____________

Story Elements–Plot

Directions: Sketch four main events from the book so far. Put them in chronological order using the flow chart below.

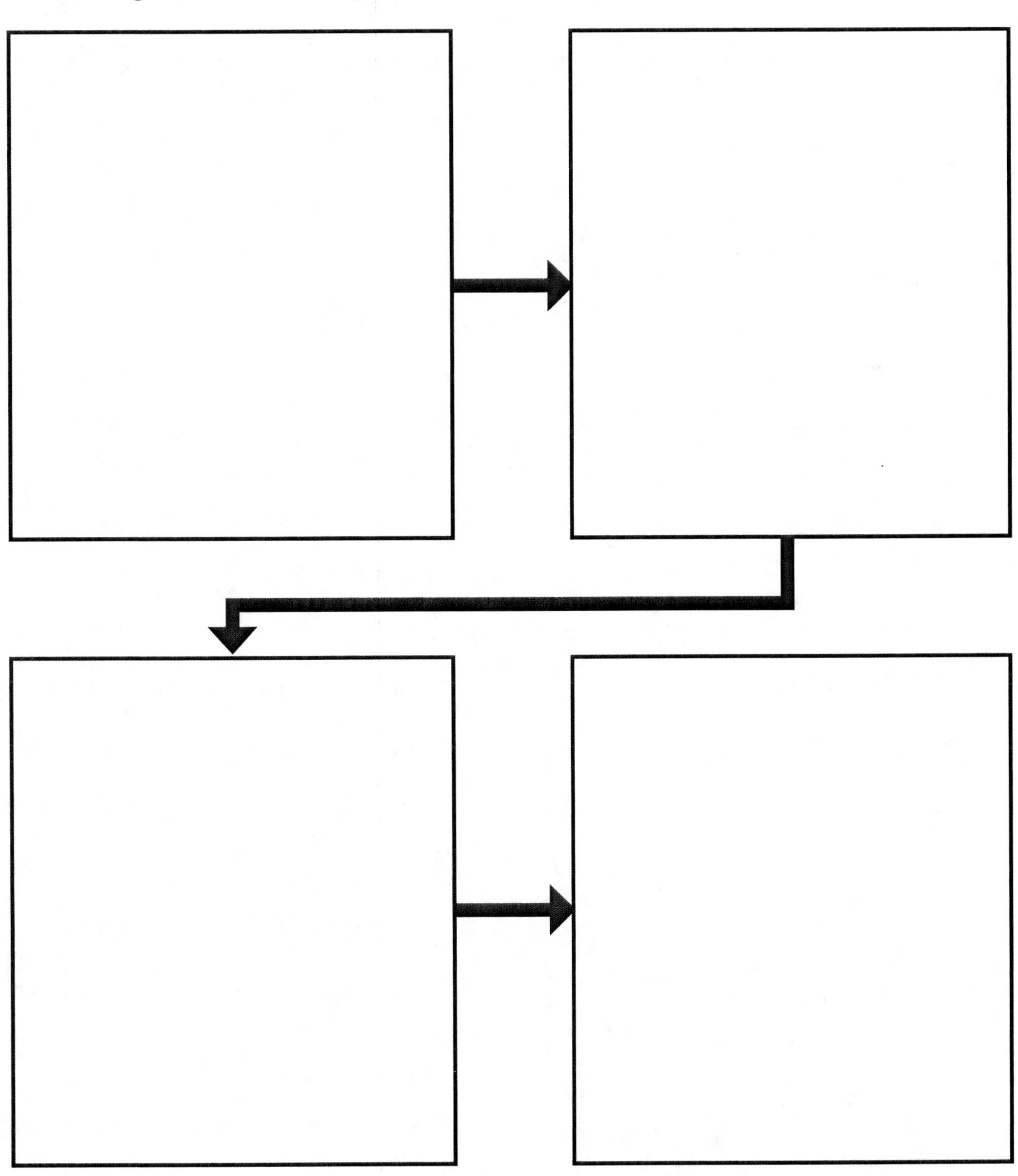

Vocabulary Overview

Key words and phrases from this section are provided below with definitions and sentences about how the words are used in the story. Introduce and discuss these important vocabulary words with students. If you think these words or other words in the story warrant more time devoted to them, there are suggestions in the introduction for other vocabulary activities (page 5).

Word	Definition	Sentence about Text
hailstones (ch. 9)	pellets of ice	The dogs eat the **hailstones** once the storm stops.
groom (ch. 9)	to make neat or tidy	Seal **grooms** herself the morning after the storm.
ax (ch. 9)	a tool with a blade at the end of a handle	Caleb uses an **ax** to chop firewood.
reins (ch. 9)	leather straps attached to a horse, allowing the driver control	Sarah holds the **reins** before pulling away in the wagon.
stern (ch. 9)	firm, strict, or harsh	Sarah speaks **sternly** to Jack before leaving for town.
murmur (ch. 9)	to speak in a low voice; to mumble	Papa **murmurs**, "Very good," as Sarah drives off in the wagon.
squint (ch. 9)	to look with the eyes partially closed	Papa **squints** at the children when they question Sarah's intentions.
wail (ch. 9)	to cry heavily; very mournful	Caleb happily **wails** when Sarah returns from town.
peer (ch. 9)	to look; to peek	Caleb **peers** into the box Anna unwraps.
preacher (ch. 9)	a person whose job is to preach the gospel	Papa will tell the **preacher** that he wants Sarah to be his wife.

Name ______________________ Date ____________

Vocabulary Activity

Directions: Practice your vocabulary and writing skills. Write at least three sentences using words from the story. Make sure your sentences show what the words mean.

Words from the Story

hailstones	groom	ax	reins	stern
squint	wail	peer	preacher	murmur

____

____

____

____

____

____

____

____

Directions: Answer this question.

1. Why does Sarah speak **sternly** to Jack before she grabs the **reins**?

____

____

Analyzing the Literature

Provided below are discussion questions you can use in small groups, with the whole class, or for written assignments. Each question is written at two levels so you can choose the right question for each group of students. For each question, a few key points are provided for your reference as you discuss the book with students.

Story Element	Level 1	Level 2	Key Discussion Points
Setting	What is the weather like when Sarah leaves for town?	Why does Anna get emotional seeing Sarah leave in the wagon?	It is a sunny day. Anna gets emotional because she remembers another wagon on another sunny day that never returned with her mother. She doesn't want that to be the case with Sarah.
Character	What promise does Jacob keep to Sarah?	How do you think Sarah feels when Jacob keeps his promise?	Jacob keeps his promise to teach Sarah how to drive the wagon. Sarah feels trusted and respected by her soon-to-be husband.
Setting	What does Sarah wear into town?	What is significant about her choice of clothing?	Sarah wears her blue dress and yellow bonnet. Her yellow bonnet is significant because it's the same one she wore when she arrived at the prairie.
Plot	What does Sarah bring back from town?	Why are the colors of the pencils so significant?	Sarah brings a package with three colored pencils. The pencils are blue, gray, and green—the colors of the sea. These colors are what she thought was missing from her drawings.

Name ____________________ Date ____________

Reader Response

Think

Think about the best present you have ever received. How did the person who gave it to you know that you would love it?

Informative/Explanatory Writing Prompt

Describe the steps you take when you pick out presents. What are the most important things to keep in mind?

Name ______________________ Date ____________

Guided Close Reading

Closely reread the last few pages of chapter 9. Start when Caleb yells "Dust!"

Directions: Think about these questions. In the chart, write ideas or draw pictures as you think. Be ready to share your answers.

1. What text shows how Caleb tries to hide his emotions when Sarah returns?
2. Use the text to tell what Caleb means by, "Sarah has brought the sea!"
3. Find evidence to support the truth in Sarah's statement, "I will always miss my old home, but the truth of it is I would miss you more."

Name ____________________ Date ____________

Making Connections–Planning a Wedding

Directions: Make a list describing Jacob and Sarah's wedding. Think about the location, guests, food, entertainment, and decorations. At the bottom of the page, draw a detailed picture of the wedding. Be sure to include everything you mentioned in your list.

________________________ ________________________

________________________ ________________________

________________________ ________________________

Name ______________________ Date ____________

Language Learning–Parts of Speech

Directions: Caleb is worried that he has driven Sarah away because he is "loud and pesky." Nobody is perfect, and Sarah loves Caleb. How would you describe yourself? What do you think you look like to others? Write five sentences about yourself. Then, circle the nouns in your sentences and underline the verbs in your sentences.

Language Hints!

- Nouns name people, places, things, or ideas.
- Verbs are action words.

- ____

  ____
- ____

  ____
- ____

  ____
- ____

  ____
- ____

  ____

Name ______________________ Date ____________

Story Elements–Setting

Directions: Illustrate what the prairie looks like at the beginning of chapter 9. On the bottom half of the paper, draw what the prairie looks like at the end of chapter 9.

Beginning of the Chapter

End of the Chapter

Name ______________________ Date ____________

Story Elements–Plot

Directions: What would you buy if you had the chance to go to a mall all by yourself? Make drawings of three different things you might like to buy for yourself. For each item describe why you want it.

Name ____________________ Date ____________

Post-Reading Theme Thoughts

Directions: Choose a main character from *Sarah, Plain and Tall*. Pretend you are that character. Draw a picture of a happy face or a sad face to show how the character would feel about each statement. Then explain how the character feels about each statement.

Character I Chose: ______________________________

Statement	How Do You Feel? ☺ ☹	What Does the Character Think?
It's exciting to try new things.		
Family is the most important thing in life.		
It's fun when things change in my life.		
I worry about people leaving.		

Name ______________________ Date ____________

Culminating Activity: You Are the Author!

Directions: Think about what is most important and meaningful about the book *Sarah, Plain and Tall*. Use these ideas to design a new front cover for the book. The cover of a book should give a strong first impression to readers. Draw your original cover below. On the lines below your drawing, describe your image.

____

____

____

Name ______________________ Date ____________

Culminating Activity: You Are the Author! *(cont.)*

Directions: Complete one of the *You Are the Author!* activities (pages 61–63) with a partner or on your own.

Activity 1: Add a new scene to the book! Think about a part of the book where the author did not tell you very much. You wish there were more details in the scene. Write a new scene that gives more detailed information about what the characters might do or say.

Name ______________________ Date ____________

Culminating Activity: You Are the Author! *(cont.)*

Directions: Complete one of the *You Are the Author!* activities (pages 61–63) with a partner or on your own.

Activity 2: Jacob writes an advertisement for a wife and mother to put in the newspaper. Create an advertisement about a person or thing that you want in your life. Maybe you want a new friend, family member, or pet? Be sure to include specific characteristics you're looking for.

Name ______________________ Date ____________

Culminating Activity: You Are the Author! *(cont.)*

Directions: Complete one of the *You Are the Author!* activities (pages 61–63) with a partner or on your own.

Activity 3: Write four poems. Each family member needs a personal poem written about him or her. Use details from the book to help you describe their personalities and physical traits.

____________________ ____________________ ____________________ ____________________ ____________________	____________________ ____________________ ____________________ ____________________ ____________________
____________________ ____________________ ____________________ ____________________ ____________________	____________________ ____________________ ____________________ ____________________ ____________________

Name ____________________ Date ____________

Comprehension Assessment

Directions: Fill in the bubble for the best response to each question.

Chapters 1–2

1. What phrase from the book shows Anna cares about Caleb?

Ⓐ "I would have named you troublesome."

Ⓑ "He was homely and plain."

Ⓒ "Don't get so close, Caleb. You'll heat up."

Ⓓ "I had gone to bed thinking how wretched he looked."

Chapters 3–4

2. Why does Caleb feel afraid while waiting for Sarah to arrive?

Ⓔ He doesn't want a new mother.

Ⓕ He's worried Sarah won't like them.

Ⓖ He doesn't like being alone with Anna.

Ⓗ He's worried he won't get his chores done.

Chapters 5–6

3. Whom does Sarah name the sheep after?

Ⓐ her brother

Ⓑ her parents

Ⓒ her pets

Ⓓ her aunts

Name ______________________ Date ____________

Comprehension Assessment *(cont.)*

Chapters 7–8

4. What do Maggie and Sarah have in common?

____

____

____

____

____

____

____

____

Chapter 9

5. What shows Caleb is worried about Sarah returning from town?

(A) Caleb chops the tree for firewood.

(B) Caleb cleans out the wood stove.

(C) The children feed the sheep before dinner.

(D) Caleb admits he is loud and pesky.

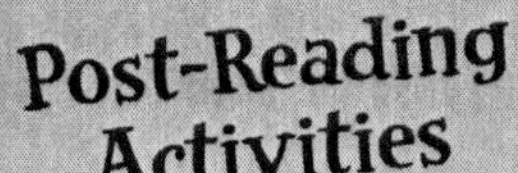

Name ____________________ Date ____________

Response to Literature: The Importance of Family

Directions: Choose a scene from the book that shows the importance of family. Think about the characters, setting, and plot in that particular scene. Draw a big, bold, colorful picture. Then, answer the questions on the next page.

Name ____________________ Date ____________

Response to Literature: The Importance of Family *(cont.)*

1. What is happening and why is this a significant scene?

____

____

____

____

2. What did you learn about the family from this scene?

____

____

____

____

3. How does this scene affect the characters for the rest of the book?

____

____

____

____

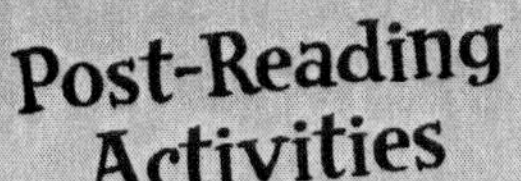

Name ____________________ Date ____________

Response to Literature Rubric

Directions: Use this rubric to evaluate student responses.

Great Job	Good Work	Keep Trying
☐ You answered all three questions completely. You included many details.	☐ You answered all three questions.	☐ You did not answer all three questions.
☐ Your handwriting is very neat. There are no spelling errors.	☐ Your handwriting can be neater. There are some spelling errors.	☐ Your handwriting is not very neat. There are many spelling errors.
☐ Your picture is neat and fully colored.	☐ Your picture is neat and some of it is colored.	☐ Your picture is not very neat and/or fully colored.
☐ Creativity is clear in both the picture and the writing.	☐ Creativity is clear in either the picture or the writing.	☐ There is not much creativity in either the picture or the writing.

Teacher Comments: ______________________________________

____

____

____

Writing Paper 2

Answer Key

The responses provided here are just examples of what students may answer. Many accurate responses are possible for the questions throughout this unit.

Vocabulary Activity—Section 1: Chapters 1–2 (page 15)

1. Sarah will be wearing a yellow **bonnet** at the train station.

Guided Close Reading—Section 1: Chapters 1–2 (page 18)

1. The sentence, "And the three of us, all smiling, went to work again," shows they are excited.
2. The paragraph starting with, "The next day . . ." describes how anxious they are waiting to hear from Sarah. It is rainy and quiet, and Anna mentions setting the table for four, instead of three.
3. Papa smiles because the end of the letter says, "Tell them I sing."

Making Connections—Section 1: Chapters 1–2 (page 19)

Check student work to make sure they include some details from the book. Examples from the book might include:

- **Prairie:** snow and ice everywhere; dirt roads; fields, grass, and sky; no close neighbors; cow ponds
- **Sea:** blue, gray, and green; foggy; flounder, sea bass, and bluefish; whales; sea birds; seals; salty; roses

Vocabulary Activity—Section 2: Chapters 3–4 (page 24)

- The wagon passes the **windmill** and the barn.
- Out in a field, a **meadowlark** sings, too.
- Papa feeds the horses as he **hitches** them up to the wagon.
- Sarah **scatters** Caleb's hair on the ground.
- Sarah's room is decorated with **blue flax** in a vase.

1. The **stalls** need to be shoveled and new hay must be laid down for the animals.

Guided Close Reading—Section 2: Chapters 3–4 (page 27)

1. Sarah scatters the hair on the ground for the birds; they will use it for their nests. She claims they can later look for the nests made of their hair.
2. Papa desperately hopes Sarah will still be around when it's time to look for the nests made of their hair. It's also a sign he believes in Sarah and her rituals.
3. Anna's relationship with Sarah is strengthening, as she thinks she looks like Sarah's daughter.

Language Learning—Section 2: Chapters 3–4 (page 29)

Anna, Caleb, dirt, horses, Maine, prairie, Russian, Sarah, shells, wagon

Vocabulary Activity—Section 3: Chapters 5–6 (page 33)

- Papa uses his **lantern** when he buries the sheep.
- Papa teaches Sarah how to **plow** the fields.
- Caleb tells Sarah about the **tumbleweeds** that come during the winter.
- Caleb runs and jumps over rocks and **gullies**.
- Sarah **wades** in the cow pond.

Guided Close Reading—Section 3: Chapters 5–6 (page 36)

1. Papa piles a bed of loose hay with his pitchfork, adding cushion to the end of the dune slide.
2. Papa and Sarah both refer to the dune as, "our dune."
3. The fact that "something is missing" from her drawing of the fields implies she is not quite settled.

Making Connections—Section 3: Chapters 5–6 (page 37)

Mammals are warm-blooded, have backbones, have fur/hair, babies feed on milk from their mothers, and they eat meat/plants.

Vocabulary Activity—Section 4: Chapters 7–8 (page 42)

1. Sarah puts on Papa's **overalls** before heading into the barn.
2. Papa says Jack is too **sly** and doesn't want Sarah riding him.
3. The chickens **shuffle** across the dirt.
4. The storm brings on a **pungent** smell and a strong wind.
5. The barn is dark and **eerie** because of the storm.

Guided Close Reading—Section 4: Chapters 7–8 (page 45)

1. Sarah is clearly frustrated and determined to speak her mind. These phrases show her emotion: "This woman wears overalls," "I want to learn how to drive the wagon. By myself," and "I am sly, too."
2. Caleb whispers, "Say no, Papa" because he is worried she will leave town.
3. Papa tries to use it as an excuse for not having time to teach her to ride and drive. She isn't willing to wait any longer and decides she can help because she knows how to fix roofs.

Vocabulary Activity—Section 5: Chapter 9 (page 51)

1. Jacob tells Sarah that Jack is sly; she wants to make sure he knows she is in charge before she takes him into town by herself.

Guided Close Reading—Section 5: Chapter 9 (page 54)

1. Caleb tries to hide his emotions by saying, "Seal was very worried!"
2. Sarah brings the colors of the sea with the colored pencils. The blue, gray, and green are the colors missing from her drawings.
3. Sarah proves she would miss them because she not only returns home safely, but gives hugs, kisses, and thinks about them by bringing back a special gift.

Comprehension Assessment (pages 64–65)

1. C. "Don't get so close, Caleb. You'll heat up."
2. F. He's worried Sarah won't like them.
3. D. her aunts
4. They both like flowers, miss where they grew up, and have kids.
5. D. Caleb admits he is loud and pesky.